Castles and Cathedrals

The Great Buildings of Medieval Times

David Hilliam

rosen central™

The Rosen Publishing Group, Inc., New York

Published in 2004 by The Rosen Publishing Group, Inc.
29 East 21st Street, New York, NY 10010

Library of Congress Cataloging-in-Publication Data

Hilliam, David.
Castles and cathedrals: the great buildings of medieval times / David Hilliam.—1st ed.
   p. cm.—(The Library of the Middle Ages)
Summary: Examines the evolution of stone architecture in the Middle Ages and the techniques of building castles and cathedrals.
Includes bibliographical references and index.
ISBN 0-8239-3990-1 (lib. bdg.)978
1. Architecture, Medieval—Juvenile literature. 2. Castles—Juvenile literature. 3. Cathedrals—Juvenile literature.
[1. Architecture, Medieval. 2. Castles. 3. Cathedrals.]
I. Title. II. Series.
NA350.H55 2003
723—dc21
                                                    2002153697

Manufactured in the United States of America

Table of Contents

1 Castle Design 5

2 Castles in Peace and War 16

3 Famous Castles in History 24

4 Cathedrals 32

5 The Great Cathedrals 44

Glossary 54

For More Information 58

For Further Reading 60

Bibliography 61

Index 62

This illustration depicts the siege of Wartburg Castle in the early fourteenth century. Attackers fire crossbows up at the castle's defenders, who (though unseen) throw boulders down on the attackers.

Castle Design

astles played a vitally important role throughout medieval Europe and were central in the lives of virtually everyone, from kings and queens to the humblest peasants. Thousands of castles were built in every country of Europe between about AD 1000 and 1550, and these were constantly being enlarged, improved, and strengthened throughout this period.

Castles were especially important in Britain after the Norman invasion. After his victory at the Battle of Hastings in 1066, the triumphant William the Conqueror (who reigned from 1066 to 1087) quickly set about occupying his new kingdom, subduing the English Saxons, and imposing Norman rule. He clearly needed fortifications on a large scale. Imagine his problem. He had very few followers, possibly only about six thousand, and he had to subdue a country of about two million people spread across a huge area.

William began to build a vast network of castles throughout the land. Each of these strongholds was occupied by a Norman lord, who held it in the name of the king. The lord was given permission to build his castle not only

Top: Defensive fortifications in the age before castle building. This is an artist's reconstruction of the ditches, earthworks, and palisades found at Old Sarum in southern England, about ten miles south of Stonehenge, a fortress typical of the Iron Age, from 600 BC to AD 43. *Center:* An artist's reconstruction of Old Sarum after the Norman invasion of AD 1066. A castle mound with a surrounding ditch has been built at the center of the fortress, and a keep has been constructed on the mound. *Bottom:* Old Sarum around AD 1140 as rebuilt by Roger, bishop of Salisbury. A more substantial castle as well as a cathedral have been constructed at the site.

as a home for himself, but also as a point of defense in his particular area, which he ruled in the name of the king. By the year 1100, at least one hundred castles had been constructed, and many more were to follow.

Motte and Bailey Castles

Before they conquered England, the Normans had already developed an effective style of fortification called the "motte and bailey" castle. The motte was a large, high mound of earth with a circular flat top. It required a great deal of hard work to dig and pile up enough earth for such an artificial hill, but when the motte was big enough a strong fortress was built on top of it. A deep ditch surrounded the motte, and a bridge crossed over the ditch to the steep steps that led up to the stronghold at the top. These early fortresses were made of wood and were cheaper, quicker, and easier to construct than stone structures.

The fort on the motte provided a safe dwelling for the lord who occupied it with his family and personal servants. However, this fort was hardly sufficient to contain everything the lord required. Another larger area was needed to accommodate everyone and everything that couldn't fit into the main fortress. This is where the bailey came in.

The bailey was an outer area below the motte, surrounded by another ditch, a rampart, and a wooden palisade, a wall made of a row of sharpened stakes. Anyone trying to force his way into the castle would first have to cross a bridge over the outer ditch before reaching the bailey gate, and then fight his way through the bailey and across another bridge over the ditch surrounding the motte. Then he would have to climb the steps up to the motte and somehow manage to force his way through another palisade at the top. After all this, he still had to get into the castle itself. It was a simple and ingenious system of defense.

Of course there were countless variations. No two castles were exactly alike. Sometimes there were two baileys (also known as wards) adjoining one motte, as at Windsor Castle. Sometimes there were even two mottes inside one bailey, as at Lincoln Castle in eastern England and at Lewes Castle near the Sussex coast. Very often a natural hill or craggy summit was used, as at Richmond Castle in Yorkshire. It was always necessary to build a castle at a strategic site, such as at the intersection of two roads or at some river crossing. The occupants of castles also needed a good supply of water, so the proper siting of castles was an extremely important matter.

Bigger and Stronger Castles

For a hundred years or so, large numbers of these motte and bailey castles were built. These early wooden castles served their immediate purpose, but they did not last long in their original state. The Norman lords were continually adding to their castles and strengthening them. Wooden fortresses quickly gave way to stone, and wooden palisades were replaced by thick stone walls, with heavier gates at the entrances.

The Middle Ages were an extremely restless age, as barons and kings were constantly quarreling. A typical example of this was when Simon de Montfort, a powerful lord in the thirteenth century, fought against King Henry III (who reigned from 1216 to 1272) and captured him and his son, Prince Edward. They were imprisoned in separate castles. Luckily for the king, Prince Edward managed to escape, raise another army, and rescue his father. Simon de Montfort was killed in the ensuing Battle of Evesham. Powerful strongholds were needed in these dangerous times, whichever side you supported.

Even a couple of centuries after the Norman invasion, there were still parts of the British Isles that were fiercely rebellious. Wales and Scotland were still fighting for their independence from the English kings. King Edward I (who reigned from 1272 to 1307), the prince who had successfully defeated Simon de Montfort in his youth, turned his attention to these troublesome regions when he became king, and in doing so he built a number of impressively strong castles to help subdue Wales.

This was also the age of the Crusades, wars in which European knights and armies tried desperately to win Jerusalem and the Holy Land from their Muslim rulers. These crusaders were impressed by the well-built stone fortresses in these eastern countries. They discovered much about designing castles from the Arabs, and they also learned new techniques for attacking and defending them. Probably the most formidable castle built by the crusaders was the immense concentric castle of Krak des Chevaliers in Syria. When the crusaders returned home, they put this new knowledge into practice as they built and enlarged their own castles. King Edward I in particular had seen the splendid fortresses in the Middle East and was keen to introduce many new designs.

The essential part of any castle is known as the keep. In the early castles, this was the wooden fort at the top of the motte. As later castles were made of stone, there was no real need for a hill. The huge central stone-built keeps were sufficiently strong in themselves. An excellent example is the Tower of London, probably the most famous castle in the world. As

An aerial view of Dover Castle in southern England clearly shows the concentric curtain walls surrounding the central keep.

soon as he was settled in England, William the Conqueror built a wooden fortress right next to a part of the old Roman wall in London. Shortly after his death, this fortress was replaced by a massively strong square stone building, known today as the White Tower, in the Tower of London. It is 90 feet (27.4 meters) tall and measures 118 feet (35.9 m) by 107 feet (32.6 m). At its base, the walls are 15 feet (4.6 m) thick, and 11 feet (3.3 m) at the top. It is a typical square Norman keep, with turrets at each of the four corners.

Another fine example of a Norman keep can be found at Dover Castle, again originally built by William the Conqueror, but replaced in the late twelfth century by the great castle

A close-up view of the central keep of Dover Castle. Note the crenellations on the battlements and the small openings for archers. Rainwater was collected from the roof.

builder King Henry II (who reigned from 1154 to 1189). It is almost 98 feet (30 m) square and 83 feet (25 m) high. Big square keeps were impressive, but the design was obviously limited and later gave way to much more complex castles.

Curtains

The old-style bailey strongholds had been surrounded by wooden palisades, but these were soon replaced by stone walls known as curtains. Similarly, the palisades surrounding the forts at the top of the mottes also began to be constructed in stone, and these were known as shell keeps. Castle builders were constantly experimenting with new designs and adapting their buildings to the contours of the land.

By the thirteenth century, the keep was no longer the main stronghold, but was incorporated into a massive stone wall that might also include many other towers. The keep at Dover was surrounded first by an inner curtain wall, then by an outer wall. As for the Tower of London, the White Tower was surrounded by two rings of encircling curtain walls with twenty separate towers built at intervals into them.

An artist's reconstruction of the central keep of the Norman castle at Scarborough, around AD 1175. A portion of the wall is cut away to show the activities on various floors. The lord's private apartments were in the keep. The lower levels were used for storage.

Concentric Castles

Concentric castles, as the name implies, had rings of defensive walls surrounding the main keep. The inner wall, with various towers built into it, was higher than the outer wall, so that defenders could shoot over the heads of those who were manning the outer defenses. Castle builders had quickly learned that square towers were more easily broken into or undermined at their corners, so later castles were given round towers.

Probably the finest concentric castle ever built was Beaumaris Castle on the Isle of Anglesey, off the north coast of Wales. It was designed for King Edward I by Master James of St. George, who has been called the greatest military architect of the age. Beaumaris was the last of his many castles, and is often considered to be his masterpiece, though sadly it was never quite finished. Only an aerial view can provide a proper understanding of its design. It consists of a huge square inner ward with massive round towers at the four corners and D-shaped towers halfway along two of its sides. On the other two sides there were gigantic gatehouses. The inner ward was surrounded by a lower wall fortified at intervals with twelve more round towers. For further safety, the entire complex was surrounded by a deep moat.

Methods of Defense

The whole point of any castle is to provide security, and designers developed many ingenious techniques to achieve this. The essential thing was to find a good site guarding a strategically important area—a seaport, a mountain pass, a valley,

This inside view of a slit window at Kenilworth Castle shows the firing steps and the tapered opening that protected archers while allowing them to fire in different directions.

a crossroad, or a major town that needed protection. Often an entire city was surrounded by a defensive wall with a castle as a part of it, as at Caernarvon Castle in northern Wales.

A water-filled moat, or at least a deep ditch, presented the first difficulty for any attacker. Rivers were deflected to fill these moats. The river Thames used to fill the moat around the Tower of London; nowadays the moat is a large grassy ditch. Entrances were always the weakest part of a castle, so these needed special protection. Drawbridges could be pulled up, making it impossible to cross the moat. Next came the gatehouse, in front of which a heavy metal door called a portcullis could be lowered, sliding along huge grooves on each side of the gatehouse walls. The gatehouse itself was usually several yards long, so after the portcullis came a tunnel at the end of which a second portcullis could be lowered. From above, defenders could easily shower boiling water, hot oil, stones, or arrows down on the attackers trapped between the two gates. Sometimes an extra walled enclosure would be constructed in front of a castle entrance. This was called a barbican. If attackers did manage to get inside the first gate of the barbican, they would be trapped inside this enclosure, again with disastrous consequences.

Tops of castle walls and towers were often crenellated, that is, fitted with battlements, raised walls with intervening open spaces, making it easy to shoot and hide. Later castle battlements were designed with machicolations, stone projections with openings so that defenders could hurl missiles on their enemies.

Castle windows were simply long vertical slits, with very narrow openings on the outer side of the walls, making it difficult to shoot into them. The openings widened toward the inside of the wall, so that defenders could fire outward in many directions. Finally, spiral staircases inside the towers usually twisted round to the right (clockwise going upward). Attackers coming up, with swords in their right hands, were therefore at a disadvantage, whereas defenders (coming down) could swing their swords more freely.

Castles in Peace and War

During the Middle Ages there were about 2,000 castles in Britain, 10,000 in France, 10,000 in Germany, and many thousands more throughout Europe. In Britain the lords who lived in them were accountable to the king, who granted them "license to crenellate." In other words, he allowed them to construct fortified buildings with battlements.

Just as castles varied in size, the lords who lived in them varied in importance. Often a small castle was no stronger than a country house where a local baron and his lady lived with just a few servants. More powerful barons and earls lived in much grander castles, and these supported fair-sized communities, more like little self-contained townships.

The most important place in any castle was the great hall, in which the lord ate his meals and entertained guests. There were always visitors to welcome. Sometimes even the king himself might suddenly arrive, together with scores of attendants all needing to be fed and accommodated. For this reason, the next most important place was the kitchen, filled with busy cooks and scullions, or kitchen helpers. Butlers and pantlers were in charge of

From the fifteenth-century manuscript *Chronicles of England*, by Jean de Wavrin, this illustration depicts the siege of Rihobane. Longbows and a primitive cannon can be seen in the picture. On the left, the attackers are using a siege tower.

buying and storing the food and drink, and ewerers provided clean table linens for the lord's table. Day and night, winter and summer, fires were needed in the kitchen, and servants had to find plenty of logs and firewood to burn.

In larger castles, even in peacetime, a force of foot soldiers and archers were always on the alert in case of attack, and of course their equipment—longbows, crossbows, pikes, and staves—had to be stored and maintained. Grooms and stable boys looked after the horses, while blacksmiths were ready to replace horseshoes whenever necessary. Bedrooms were

An aerial view of the ruins of Framlingham Castle in eastern England shows the curtain wall around the castle mound.

organized according to their importance by a marshal who was in charge of many pages and maids. Supervising all the servants within the castle's household was the most important figure of all—the steward, who was directly answerable to the lord himself for everything that went on in the building. There were also reeves and bailiffs who managed the lord's farms and collected rents.

This is an interior room of Richmond Castle in Yorkshire in northern England. Though tapestries and other wall hangings would have softened the appearance of such rooms, they were still dark, drafty, and cold places in which to live.

The lady of the castle needed her personal servants, including clerks who knew how to read and keep accounts, and nurses and tutors to look after her children. Then there were spinners and weavers making clothes and soft furnishings, and we mustn't forget the launderers who washed everything, either in great wooden tubs or in a nearby river. It's almost impossible to list all the people who might have lived and worked in one castle, sometimes throughout their entire working lives. There were armorers, wheelwrights, carpenters, priests, and candlemakers. There were often visiting jugglers, acrobats, jesters, and minstrels who wandered from castle to castle, entertaining the occupants in exchange for food and lodging.

Probably the worst job of all was that of the gong farmer, whose smelly task was to clear out the castle's gongs, or toilets—deep pits filled with excrement. Everyone had his or her necessary part to play in making the castle run smoothly, even the poor old keeper of the gongs!

An illustration from a fourteenth-century German Bible depicts the building of the Tower of Babel. Medieval techniques for lifting stones are shown.

Castles at War

Medieval warfare involved not only great battles such as those at Hastings and Agincourt, but also and more frequently, long drawn-out sieges in which an attacking army surrounded a town and its castle, forced their surrender, and then moved on to the next center of resistance.

Castles preparing for a siege needed to amass as much food, fuel, and ammunition as possible. Farm animals were brought into the castle wards. Archers had to make plenty of arrows, and everyone stockpiled rocks and stones to hurl at the enemy. Naturally, the attacking army tried their utmost to gain entry, and many siege engines were invented. Battering rams were used to break down doors and any weak parts of the castle walls. These were trundled up to the walls on wheels, and they had a covered roof to ward off missiles being showered down from above. Siege towers, sometimes three or four stories high, also on wheels, were drawn up to the castle battlements so that the attackers could leap onto the walls. European knights had learned how to make and use siege towers at the siege of Jerusalem in 1099 during the First Crusade.

A popular technique was to undermine the castle. Tunnels were dug beneath the walls. The tunnel roof was propped up with wooden beams, and when these were set on fire, the roof collapsed, bringing the castle wall down with it. Wooden siege engines called trebuchets were invented to fling rocks into the castle. They were gigantic slings. A pivoting arm had a heavy counterweight at one end, and when this was suddenly dropped, the long arm swung over and the missile was hurled toward its target. Sometimes severed heads of captured prisoners or even stinking animal corpses were utilized as ammunition. A similar device called a mangonel used twisted rope to fling missiles. Another weapon was the ballista, which could shoot massive javelins. It worked in the same way as schoolchildren use rulers to flick pellets, but on a much larger scale. A huge lever was drawn back, and when it was released, it sprang forward and shot its spear with incredible speed and force.

However, no weapon was ever as effective as hunger. Unless outside help could arrive, the occupants of a besieged castle were usually doomed to die, if not by siege weapons, then sooner or later by starvation. If prisoners were taken during a siege, they were usually flung into windowless cellars, often mere pits without any means of escape. These were called oubliettes from a French word meaning "to forget." They were simply forgotten and left to rot in their own filth.

Gunpowder and cannons, introduced in the fourteenth century, eventually made all these weapons obsolete. In the face of terrifying bombardments by cannonballs, castles themselves became increasingly out of date after about 1500.

WESTERN EUROPE
DURING THE
MIDDLE AGES

SCOTLAND

ENGLAND
London

HOLY ROMAN
EMPIRE

Normandy

Paris

KINGDOM OF
FRANCE

Aquitaine   Burgundy

Rome

KINGDOM OF
SPAIN

ITALY

KINGDOM
OF
PORTUGAL

Mediterranean
Sea

SICILY

AFRICA

Famous Castles in History

As we have mentioned, the Tower of London was one of England's most famous castles. It was begun by William the Conqueror and was enlarged by many later kings, particularly Henry III and Edward I, who encircled the original White Tower with a ring of nineteen additional towers. Over the centuries it has acted as fortress, palace, storehouse, arsenal, treasury, mint, prison, and even a royal menagerie. Famous prisoners kept here include Queen Elizabeth I, when she was still a princess, and two of Henry VIII's wives, who were both later beheaded. It has been the scene of torture and murders. Henry VI and Edward V were both assassinated here. It even held Adolf Hitler's deputy, Rudolf Hess, during World War II. For centuries it has held the crown jewels, now permanently on display in a dazzling exhibition.

Windsor Castle was also begun by William the Conqueror and has been added to many times over the centuries. The Round Tower was originally a Norman keep, and from the air it's easy to see that it was a motte with two baileys. Windsor is still in use as a royal palace. It's a castle that has been lived in for nine and a half centuries.

One of England's most famous castles, the Tower of London was a Norman fortress begun by William the Conqueror. This aerial view shows the central keep, the curtain walls, and the Tower Bridge, which spans the Thames River.

The British royal family is frequently in residence, as it is conveniently only about twenty miles west of London. However, visitors can look round much of it and admire the spectacular furnishings and objects on display.

Dover Castle is situated on the southeast coast of England, guarding the English Channel at its narrowest crossing point. In fact, you can actually see France from Dover Castle, which possesses an enormous complex of walls and towers and medieval tunnels burrowing below them. The Romans had a fort here nine hundred years before the Normans, and it wasn't until almost nine hundred years after that, in 1956, that the British army finally gave up using it. The Norman keep, built for Henry II between 1181 and 1188, is especially impressive. More tunnels were added during the World War II to contain a hospital and a military command center in case of invasion by Nazi Germany.

Other famous English castles are at Alnwick in Northumberland, Warwick near Shakespeare's birthplace in central England, and Carisbrooke on the Isle of Wight, where Charles I was held prisoner while waiting to be executed. During the English Civil War (1642–1651), Oliver Cromwell, the lord protector, blew up many of Britain's castles. Examples of these spectacular ruins are Corfe Castle in Dorset, Kenilworth Castle in Warwickshire, and Wolvesey Castle in Winchester.

Scottish and Welsh Castles

Edinburgh Castle is perched high on a rocky crag overlooking Scotland's capital city. The last king to live there was James VI of Scotland, who became James I of England (who reigned from

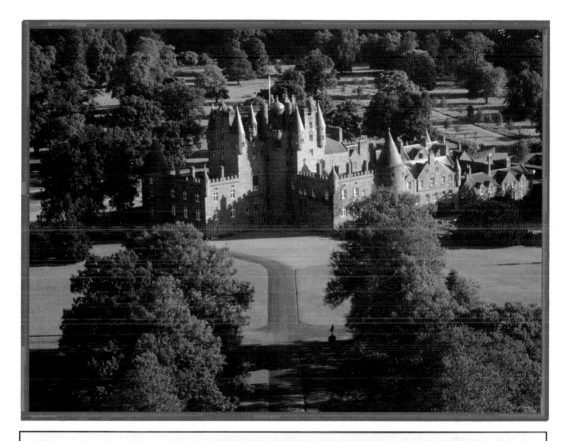

Glamis Castle in Scotland was the home of Macbeth, who was the king of Scotland from 1040 to 1057 and the subject of Shakespeare's famous play.

1603 to 1625) after the death of Queen Elizabeth I (who reigned from 1558 to 1603). James's mother, Mary Queen of Scots, gave birth to him in a tiny room there. Today, in an adjoining room, the beautiful Scottish crown jewels are displayed. Glamis Castle, home of Macbeth (king of Scotland from 1040 to 1057) and the birthplace of Queen Elizabeth II's mother, is still lived in. From the battlements of Stirling Castle can be seen the Wallace Memorial, commemorating William Wallace and his victory over the English at Stirling Bridge in 1297.

This photograph of Caerphilly Castle in southern Wales shows the central keep, the curtain wall, and the gatehouse. Built by Baron Gilbert de Clare, it is the largest castle in Great Britain.

In Wales, the English king Edward I was determined to break the power of the Welsh lords. He succeeded, and to keep the peace he ordered a series of castles to be built at strategic points. A brilliant military architect, Master James of St. George, designed and built these castles, each of which is a masterpiece of castle construction. They are to be found at Flint, Rhuddlan, Conwy (sometimes spelled Conway), Harlech, Aberystwith, Caernarvon, and Beaumaris. Wales is a very mountainous, rocky area, and stone building materials were close at hand. Caerphilly Castle in southern Wales has been described as the greatest castle in the British Isles.

An aerial view of Beaumaris Castle, on the island of Anglesey in northern Wales, shows both inner and outer curtain walls and the central keep.

Certainly it is the largest, covering thirty acres, almost twice the area of the Tower of London. It was built by an independent baron, Gilbert de Clare, who probably didn't ask royal permission to build it. However, Edward I was pleased to see this castle going up, adding to his own series of fortifications in Wales.

French Castles

Castles are to be found everywhere in France. William the Conqueror himself was born in the castle of Falaise in Normandy. Carcasone, a fortified town in the south of France, has inner and outer walls with fifty towers and a moat. Avignon, also in the south, has a fine fortress-palace, built for medieval popes. Some of the finest castles are on the Loire River in central France and are splendid examples of how, in the late Middle Ages, castles were turned into sumptuous stately homes, called chateaux, for French noblemen. Especially noteworthy is the castle at Chinon, where Joan of Arc persuaded the French king to let her lead the French armies against the English. The castles at Chambord and Chamberry are famous for their beauty.

German Castles

Strategically and commercially, the Rhine River is one of the most important rivers in Europe. Scores of castles were built along both banks, either on rocky summits or by the riverside. Many are very small but extremely picturesque. A famous Rhine castle is the one at Pfalzrafenstein, a curious hexagonal building standing on an island in the middle of the river, built in 1327 as a toll station by a local ruler. Some of these Rhine castles now contain hotels or museums. Other splendid German castles, not on the Rhine, are at Heidelberg, Meissen, and Rothenburg. Rothenburg is probably the finest surviving medieval fortified town in Europe.

Spanish Castles

Spanish castles were built or influenced by the Moors, the Islamic peoples who ruled Spain during the Middle Ages. Three impressive examples are the Alcazar of Segovia, called a *gran buque*, a "great ship," because of its long shape; El Real de Manzanares, north of Madrid; and the Alhambra, near

The Alcazar, in Segovia, Spain, was constructed in the fifteenth century by Spain's Moorish rulers. The Moors were Muslim invaders from North Africa who ruled Spain for seven hundred years, until the late fifteenth century.

Grenada, the last Moorish stronghold to be recaptured by the Christians in 1492.

With the invention of gunpowder, castles ceased to be defensible and lost their importance. In any case, nobles were beginning to want more luxurious homes. Old-style castles were horribly cold and drafty. After the sixteenth century, many castles were either blown up, abandoned, or transformed into mansions and large stately homes.

Cathedrals

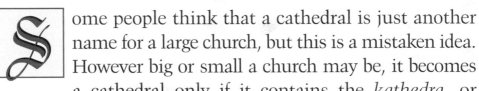

ome people think that a cathedral is just another name for a large church, but this is a mistaken idea. However big or small a church may be, it becomes a cathedral only if it contains the *kathedra*, or bishop's chair, the throne from which the bishop exercises his authority. "Kathedra" is simply the Greek word for "seat." The area over which a bishop rules is called a diocese, another Greek-derived word meaning "household." Another name for a diocese is "see," which derives from *sedes*, the Latin word for "seat." Church words often come from the ancient worlds of Greece and Rome, the worlds of the first Christians.

In those very early centuries, Christians were persecuted and often killed for their faith. They had to meet secretly in their own houses. But when their religion became officially recognized, they were able to worship and gather in larger meeting places, and the most suitable buildings were the Roman basilicas, or law courts, which were long rectangular buildings. One end was semicircular, containing a platform for the chair of the most important person present.

It was only natural that when Christians began to construct buildings especially for their religious worship they should adopt this same architectural plan. There are countless basilica-shaped cathedrals in southern Europe, with a bishop's chair in the apse, the name we give to the basilica's rounded end. In northern Europe, however, and especially in Britain, square-ended cathedrals were more common.

One essential feature in building churches and cathedrals was that they needed to be properly oriented. This means that the altar should always have been at the eastern end, facing the rising sun. "Orient" means "eastern," derived from a Latin word meaning "to rise." Orientation was both practical and symbolic. It meant that the most important part of the building was flooded with early-morning light, and it also represented the rising of Jesus Christ from the dead.

The first cathedrals were quite small. As Christianity became more firmly established, cathedrals became larger and more complex in design. It soon became the practice to make them cruciform, that is, cross-shaped. Sometimes, in the earlier centuries, the four arms of the cross were the same size, but usually the arms built on the north and south sides were smaller, so that the ground plan of the cathedral very much resembled the actual cross on which Jesus died. Such symbolism was important.

Romanesque Cathedrals in England

From about AD 600 to 1200, a style of building was developed that was known as Romanesque. As the name suggests, it was based on the architecture of classical Rome, with strong

Castles and Cathedrals

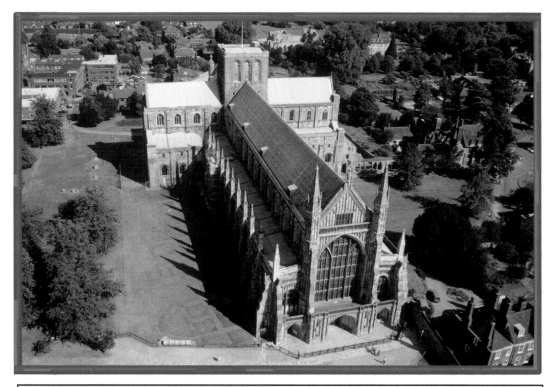

Winchester was the ancient Saxon capital of England. When William the Conqueror seized the town, he had the Saxon cathedral torn down and this magnificent Norman cathedral built in its place. This photograph shows the western facade, the northern and southern transepts creating the cruciform shape, and the long nave—the longest Gothic nave in Europe.

round-headed arches and powerful, heavy columns holding up the roofs of buildings. This was the style used by the Normans, who introduced it to England after 1066. Because of this, it is often referred to as Norman architecture, though strictly speaking it was a style that was common throughout Europe.

The Normans were great builders. They filled Britain with castles. As a part of his program to dominate his new kingdom, William the Conqueror set about creating new dioceses and reorganizing the boundaries of existing ones. It was a political and practical necessity to dominate, even in church matters. He and his successors built on a massive scale to impress everyone that they had come to stay.

Winchester was the ancient capital of England, home of the Saxon kings, and inevitably William the Conqueror made it one of his headquarters. Its Saxon cathedral was ruthlessly pulled down, and a huge Norman replacement cathedral was built right next to where it had been. Today, Winchester Cathedral still stands, with its strong round Norman arches, an enduring example of Norman architecture. It is one of the largest cathedrals in England and the longest Gothic church in Europe with a length of 556 feet (169 m).

About thirty miles west of Winchester is an old Saxon hill fort known today as Old Sarum. It was a good site for a defensive castle. William not only built a fortress there, but he also built a new cathedral, requiring the bishop of Sherborne to move there. Thus Sherborne lost its cathedral status, and a new diocese of Sarum came into existence. It was easier to keep an eye on, as it was closer to Winchester, and William made Osmund, his cousin, its bishop. In a marshy area near present-day Cambridge, William the Conqueror had encountered much fierce opposition. A part of his response was to build an impressive new cathedral there, at Ely. Its gigantic Norman tower is a statement of power.

In the north, near the Scottish border and far from Winchester and London, the Normans built their masterpiece, Durham Cathedral. It has been called the finest Romanesque church in Europe. It acted as a great fortress-cathedral with a formidable castle standing nearby. Its bishop was given special authority to rule the north on behalf of the king, with power to raise his own private army. Such a powerful figure needed this

An interior view of the nave at Winchester Cathedral. It is 556 feet (169 m) long.

impressive cathedral, begun in 1093, to replace the much smaller existing building.

Durham Cathedral is so splendid that modern filmmakers have used it for unusual sets. The cathedral authorities even gave permission for some scenes from *Harry Potter and the Sorcerer's Stone* to be filmed there. Inside, the massive pillars are about 7 feet (2 m) in diameter and are deeply carved with geometric patterns. Outside, the cathedral guards a natural steep-sided peninsula surrounded on three sides by a river. For the Normans, the site of this cathedral was strategically important. In fact, in a later century, it was used briefly to imprison captured Scottish rebels.

Gothic Cathedral Design

At the end of the twelfth century in northern France, a striking new style of architecture was introduced, which later became known as Gothic. Notre Dame Cathedral in Paris was one of the first constructed in this style. It was begun in 1163.

The main and immediately obvious difference between Gothic and the older Romanesque architecture was the introduction of the pointed arch for windows, doorways, and arcades, that is, rows of arches. This may seem a very simple change, but the implications were extremely important for two reasons. First, a pointed arch is much more versatile in spanning a given space than a round one. A round arch has to complete a half circle, but a pointed one can bridge any distance by making the point more or less sharply angled. Second, a pointed arch is stronger, and so an architect can build higher and lighter walls incorporating tall pointed windows called lancets, which are high, narrow, and pointed.

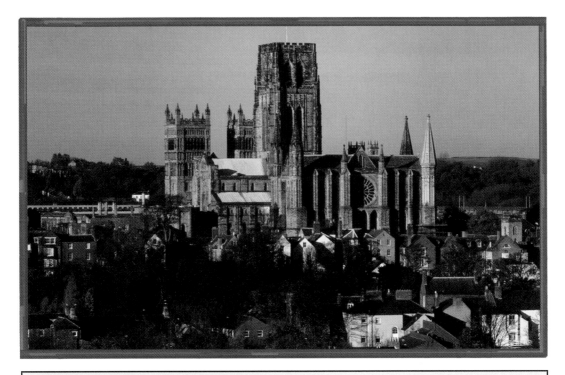

Durham Cathedral, in northern England near the Scottish border, is considered the finest Romanesque cathedral in all of Europe.

This discovery by French architects quickly spread throughout northern France, England, and the rest of Europe. Some of the greatest French Gothic cathedrals are at Rouen, Amiens, Chartres, Beauvais, and Rheims. The new style was often introduced as an addition to cathedrals that were already in the process of being built, and later whole new cathedrals were constructed in this style.

In 1220 in England, a wonderful opportunity occurred when a brand-new cathedral was being planned at Salisbury. At Old Sarum, the hill fort where William the Conqueror had built a castle and a new cathedral, it was clear that the site was too small. So it was decided to move the entire town into the valley below and build a new cathedral in what would be New

Sarum, present-day Salisbury. No cathedral has ever been built so quickly or so consistently in one style as this one in Salisbury. It is a marvel of the new design, acknowledged as one of the most beautiful buildings in the world. Certainly it is the most perfect example of the early English Gothic style.

Salisbury Cathedral has pointed arches in all its doors, windows, and arcades. Tall single lancet windows are grouped in threes and fives, creating a beautiful effect. The overall design is cruciform, with not just one pair of transepts (the "arms" of the cross), but also with a second smaller pair nearer the square eastern end.

Typically, the central body of a medieval Gothic cathedral, the nave, is flanked by aisles that extend the overall width. Built over the aisles is a windowless gallery called a triforium high up along the sides of the nave. Above this comes the clerestory, a row of windows letting in plenty of light. The whole of this comprises a galaxy of pointed arches and lancet windows.

Cathedrals built to such heights demanded strong support. This led to the other crucially important invention of the new Gothic style, flying buttresses on the exterior walls. These were huge stone prop-arches, with the top ends set against and supporting a high inner main wall and the lower end supported by a lower outer wall of an aisle. This daring architectural device is both practical and visually beautiful. The eastern exterior of Notre Dame in Paris is a supreme example.

In quick succession during the thirteenth and fourteenth centuries, other Gothic cathedrals were built or extended throughout Europe. However, no cathedral except Salisbury was built solely in the early English style.

Aud en ainsi de quan · ure diuant dit · Quaud salomo
tes uertus et de quants · son fil: aucores iceune enfant eut
biens il a este aucteur · prins le royaume de son pre. et fu
a ceulx de sa lignee. et · assis ou siege royal. tout le peuple

This fifteenth-century manuscript illumination shows a multitude of workmen busy constructing a cathedral.

The flying buttresses at Chartres Cathedral, built in the thirteenth century. These huge, arching stone structures enabled medieval builders to provide additional support for the high stone walls of churches.

Decorated and Perpendicular Gothic

Styles are always changing, and the Gothic style went through three periods of development, each taking roughly a century. The first of these periods, from about AD 1150 to 1250, is known as early English, when the style was simple, bold, and often rather plain.

The second period, from about AD 1250 to 1350, known as decorated, involved a much greater elaboration of patterns in the stonework at the tops of windows, known as tracery, with simple geometric shapes at first and then with more flowing shapes. Also at this time the masons added a great deal of imaginative carvings almost everywhere. Parts of the cathedrals in York, Ely, Exeter, Lincoln, and Wells show this decorated style.

The final period, from about AD 1350 to 1450, is known as perpendicular, because by then the architects had become skilled at designing gigantic windows in which there were numerous mullions, or vertical divisions between the panes,

A stained-glass window in Chartres Cathedral. Stained glass as an art form flourished during the age of cathedral building. The panels usually told biblical stories, which could be understood by those who were illiterate.

going from top to bottom, creating powerful perpendicular effects. Perpendicular patterns were predominant in this final phase, and the creative, intricate carvings of the decorated period became increasingly rare.

The reason for this is that in the middle of the fourteenth century, the bubonic plague killed off huge number of workers throughout Europe. As there were fewer masons, it was quicker and cheaper to mass-produce straightforward patterns rather than to take the time to make up elaborate designs. The Black Death arrived in England in 1348, at the beginning of the perpendicular period. Buildings after this date are often impressive, but the designs are somewhat repetitive. However, by then all the great medieval cathedrals had already been built. So the perpendicular style is usually found in additional extensions, as in Winchester, or in great chapels that were not cathedrals, such as at King's College, Cambridge, or St. George's Chapel, Windsor.

An important point to make about medieval cathedrals is that they usually took many years to complete, and you will often see parts built in different periods and styles right next to each other. The medieval builders did not mind mixing styles. The early English cathedral at Salisbury, for example, had a decorated spire built onto it in the following century, and the eleventh-century Norman nave of Winchester Cathedral was encased in perpendicular stonework in the fourteenth century. Such variation adds interest today as we study cathedrals and try to work out when each part was built. There are many points of style to look out for, but the elaboration of the window tracery usually gives the best clue.

The Great Cathedrals

All cathedrals were busy centers of activity. Every single day throughout many centuries, people prayed and worshiped in these great buildings, from the day they were consecrated, or blessed and dedicated to God. Clearly a large number of people were needed to support the activity of worship and service to the community.

The bishop's task was to look after the whole of his diocese, with all its parishes, churches, and clergy. It was not the duty of the bishop to look after the cathedral. He delegated this role to the dean, who was not only in charge of the building but also of a group of clergy known as canons, who helped lead the services. Forming a governing body of the cathedral, the canons were collectively known as the chapter. In every cathedral there is a chapter house where the dean and chapter formerly met to discuss cathedral matters.

Music has always been an important feature of Christian worship, so choirs were formed early on, consisting of men and boy choristers. Leading the choir was the choirmaster, but the cathedral official in charge of managing all the services, including the music, was called the precentor. Many helpers and workers were needed to clean and maintain the building and its possessions. A cathedral was served by a large community of people dedicating their lives in different ways to God.

Parts of a Cathedral

From the outside, the most elaborate feature of a cathedral is usually the western facade, which is often filled with niches displaying statues of saints. The cathedrals at Wells and Salisbury are good examples of this. In France there are often three deeply recessed doorways on the western front, containing intricate carvings of biblical scenes. Above each door is a space called the tympanum, which can also be filled with fascinating carvings, as at Notre Dame in Paris and at Chartres. Most medieval people couldn't read, so these carvings were important to help teach them the Christian message.

Almost all Gothic cathedrals possess a tower or spire, sometimes both, and sometimes several. Frequently there are twin towers or spires at the western end, with another taller tower or spire at the crossing formed at the intersection of the nave and transepts. Height is a particular feature of Gothic architecture, and there may be many pointed finials, or decorative spirelike decorations, on the tops of buttresses. The builders were always wanting to point upward to heaven.

Inside, the nave is the main body of the cathedral, and running parallel with the nave, separated from it by a row of pillars, are aisles on each side. Beyond the crossing, the nave usually narrows, and this area is called the choir, where the clergy and choristers hold the services. The choir almost always has beautifully carved wooden choir stalls. Behind the altar there may be a round apse, perhaps with several small chapels built around the semicircular ambulatory, where one can walk around behind the altar from one side to the other. Often there are a number of chapels built into the nave and transepts, each with a special purpose and dedicated to different saints.

There is also a chapter house, already mentioned, often octagonal in shape, with seats for the clergy all around it. There may be a crypt underneath the building, containing yet more altars and chapels. Just outside one of the cathedral walls may be a cloister, which is a square walking area, roofed all around, but with an open center. Some cathedrals have a bell tower, called a campanile, a little distance from the main building. There is a good example at Chichester, but the most famous is the Leaning Tower of Pisa. Most English cathedrals are surrounded with a spacious area known as a close, often with large lawns and with houses often dating from medieval times.

Medieval cathedrals are treasure-houses of beautiful works of art. Stained-glass windows with pictures of Bible stories and saints shed colored light into the building. Chartres Cathedral in France and Canterbury Cathedral in England have splendid examples. Then there are carvings in wood and stone everywhere, especially on the capitals, the tops of pillars, and in the choir stalls. Often there are interesting carved wooden misericords hidden underneath hinged seats. Other places to look for carvings are the font, used for baptisms; the pulpit, from which sermons are preached; and the lectern, which holds the Bible. It's always worth looking into hidden corners, too. Every cathedral also has interesting items from its past—old clocks showing the sun and moon, military banners, statues, ancient maps, and heraldic coats of arms.

From a historical point of view, the tombs are probably the most important feature of cathedrals. You will often find effigies of kings, noblemen, and other famous people, and in many cathedrals there are shrines of saints. Medieval pilgrims traveled long distances to pray at these shrines, and they brought great wealth to the cathedrals. In England, one of the most famous shrines, now destroyed, was the tomb of St. Thomas Becket at Canterbury. Many Catholic cathedrals still possess relics that are believed by many to be genuine fragments of items in the gospel story, such as pieces of the cross on which Jesus died.

There are often many other historical associations to be discovered. Rheims in France and Aachen in Germany have cathedrals where kings were crowned. Old St. Paul's in London was the scene of many celebrations after military victories, such as the defeat of the Spanish armada. Medieval cathedrals have witnessed so many dramatic moments in their long history that they provide us intriguing links to the past.

Famous Medieval Cathedrals

During the Middle Ages there were twenty-three cathedrals in England. Here is a complete list in order of the foundation of their dioceses: Canterbury, AD 597; St. Paul's in London, 604; Rochester, 604; York, 627; Lichfield, 656; Winchester, 662; Hereford, 676; Worcester, 680; Wells, 909; Durham, 995; Ely, 1109; Exeter, 1046; Chichester, 1075; Lincoln,

Salisbury Cathedral in southern England is famous for its wonderful spire.

1075; Salisbury, 1075; Bath, 1088; Norwich, 1094; Carlisle, 1133; and Bristol, Chester, Gloucester, Oxford, and Peterborough, all in 1542. In 1075, three new dioceses were created by William the Conqueror, and in 1542, five more dioceses were created, this time by King Henry VIII (who reigned from 1509 to 1547). Henry, having just abolished all the monasteries in the kingdom, decided to turn some of the most important abbeys into cathedrals, with bishops instead of abbots.

All the cathedrals just listed are wonderful examples of Romanesque or Gothic architecture. Each cathedral is unique, with its own special features. Winchester possesses the bones of the Saxon kings and is the longest cathedral in England. Salisbury has the tallest spire in England at 404 feet (123 m). York is built on the site of a Roman barrack square, and remains of this can be seen in its crypt. Durham possesses the bones of one of the earliest Saxon saints, St. Cuthbert. Most cathedrals were built over several centuries and were therefore constructed in a variety of different architectural styles.

France

The great burst of Gothic cathedral building in France in the twelfth and thirteenth centuries resulted in some magnificent examples of medieval architecture. Notre Dame in Paris has particularly beautiful flying buttresses and is notable for the frighteningly weird life-size carvings of devils on its western towers. The buildings at Amiens, Beauvais, Chartres, Evreux, Rheims, Rouen, and Strasbourg, all in northern France, and Albi and Bourges in the south are among the finest cathedrals in France. Chartres is famed for its stained glass and also for

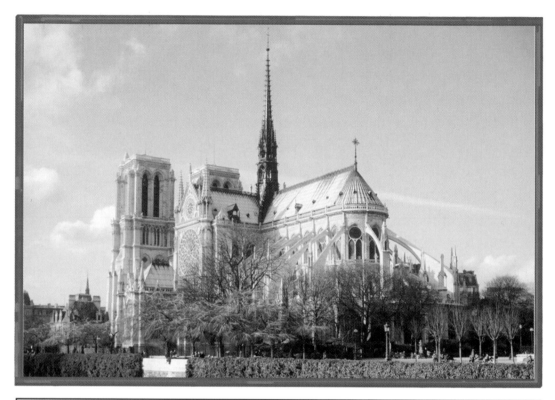

Magnificent flying buttresses are visible at the eastern end of Notre Dame Cathedral in Paris, above.

the remarkable series of external carvings around its doors. Beauvais was deliberately designed to be the tallest cathedral in the world, and its tower and spire reached 497 feet (149 m). The tower fell down in 1573, but the high nave remains.

Germany

Charlemagne (c. 742–814), the first Holy Roman emperor, ruled his empire from present-day Aachen, Germany, and his tomb lies in its cathedral. Thirty German kings were crowned there between AD 936 and 1531, and it still possesses Charlemagne's great white marble throne. The town of Freiburg im Breisgau probably has the most beautiful cathedral in southern Germany, with an extraordinarily delicate spire carved in pink stone, almost like lace. Regensburg has a splendid pair of spires on its western front, also in the lacy style of Freiburg, which is known as openwork. Ulm possesses the tallest spire in the world, reaching a staggering height of 528 feet (158 m). Cologne has one of the finest and largest cathedrals in Europe, with twin spires only 13 feet (4 m) shorter than that of Ulm's cathedral. It houses one of the most precious relics of medieval Christendom, the Shrine of the Magi (the three wise men).

Italy

There is a very different look to Italian cathedrals, partly because Renaissance styles began earlier in Italy than elsewhere, so that the elaborate Gothic style found in other European cathedrals did not develop there. Also, there is an abundance of marble in Italy, so the typical gray stone buildings in England, France, and Germany give way to cathedrals of gleaming marble, mostly white but sometimes in other colors, too. The ornate facade of the cathedral at Sienna, for example, is predominantly white, but with some red and green mixed in, and the interior has horizontal black and white strips of stone throughout. Pisa is famous for its leaning tower, the campanile. Florence has a superb cathedral, also in patterned marble, and the campanile just beside it, designed by the great artist Giotto, is brilliantly colored. Saint Mark's in Venice hardly resembles anything yet described here, because it is so heavily influenced by Eastern and Turkish styles. Milan, in

This is the western facade of the cathedral in Pisa, Italy, which was built in the twelfth century. The famous Leaning Tower of Pisa is the campanile (bell tower) for this cathedral.

northern Italy, is different again, built in the late Gothic style in white marble, with literally hundreds of pointed finials decorating its roof.

Spain

During the thirteenth century, Spanish armies managed to recapture land taken by the Moors in the eighth century. As they did so, they founded great cathedrals in their principal cities. The first of these was Burgos, begun in 1221 and founded by the king of Castile. It has intricately carved twin spires on the western front and a central tower with twelve pinnacles. Barcelona's cathedral has another splendid western front, and so does Santiago de Compostella, which attracted hundreds of thousands of pilgrims to its shrine of the apostle Saint James the Great. This pilgrimage was second in importance only to a pilgrimage to Rome during the Middle Ages. Salamanca has two noteworthy cathedrals standing side by side—a "new" one begun in 1513 and an impressive old Romanesque cathedral. However, the massive fifteenth-century cathedral in Seville is perhaps the most awesome of all, as it is the largest medieval cathedral in the world. It possesses a large monument to Christopher Columbus in the southern transept.

Every capital city and major town in Europe has its cathedral, and it would be impossible to list them all. In Austria, there is Saint Stephen's in Vienna, with its brilliantly colored and patterned roof. Saint Vitus's Cathedral in Prague, in the Czech Republic, contains the tomb of Saint Wenceslas. In Holland, the cathedral of Saint John in S'Hertogenbosch has swarms of curious carved creatures scrambling up the flying buttresses, apparently trying to escape from demons. The crucial point to make is that every cathedral is unique.

Glossary

ambulatory   The area at the rounded end of a basilica-shaped cathedral. It comes from the Latin word *ambulare,* meaning "to walk."

apse   The rounded end of a cathedral built in the shape of a basilica.

arcade   A row of arches, either round or pointed, often used to support a roof.

bailey   The outer area below the motte of an early Norman castle, surrounded by a defensive wall.

bailiff   A castle servant who dealt with outlying lands and property of the lord.

barbican   A stone structure built in front of a castle's entrance with an outer door or gateway. This provided the first point of defense.

basilica   A church, usually with a rounded eastern end. This Greek word was originally used to mean "law court," and its shape is derived from that of the law courts in ancient Greece and Rome.

Black Death   The name given to the great plague, which ravaged Europe between 1348 and 1351, killing about one-eighth of the population.

butler   An important servant in a castle, in charge of buying and storing food and drink and also in charge of the inferior servants.

buttress   A thicker, vertical part of a wall, added to give strength.

campanile   The clock tower of a cathedral.

chapel   A separate small area for worship, with its own altar, in a cathedral.

cloister   A covered rectangular walkway adjoining a cathedral, with an open space in the middle.

close   The area around an English cathedral, often with lawns and trees immediately around the cathedral.

concentric castle   A castle designed with one or more rings of defensive walls.

crenellation   The serrated or toothed upper battlements of a castle wall, designed to provide protected firing positions for castle defenders.

crossing   The square area in the middle of a cathedral where the nave and the transepts meet.

cruciform   Cross-shaped; the ground plan of a cathedral is usually cruciform, with transepts forming the arms.

crypt   An area beneath a cathedral.

curtain   An outer or inner defensive stone wall around a castle, often incorporating a series of towers.

effigy   On a tomb, a life-size representation of the person buried there, shown lying down. It is, in fact, a horizontal statue.

finial   A tall decorative feature, like a miniature spire.

flying buttress   A stone arch acting as a prop on the exterior of a cathedral, providing support for the high walls.

gongs "Privies" or primitive pits that served as a castle's toilets. The person who cleaned them out was called the gong farmer.

groom A servant who looked after horses.

keep The large square central fortress in a castle; the Norman name for a keep was donjon, from which the word "dungeon" is derived.

lancet window A single tall window with a pointed gothic top.

machicolation A projection jutting out from the top of a castle wall or tower, designed to allow the defenders to drop things onto attackers.

mangonel A kind of catapult using twisted rope as a means of flinging rocks into a castle.

misericord A small projection on the bottom of a church seat that provides support when a worshiper stands.

motte A large circular man-made mound of earth, upon which an early Norman castle was built.

nave The main body of a cathedral, always orientated east–west. The word is derived from the Latin word *navis*, meaning "ship." The shape of the roof beams looks like a ship turned upside down.

palisade The defensive wall surrounding the bailey of an early Norman castle, usually made of sharpened wooden stakes.

pointed arch An arch or opening that comes to a point at the top, rather than a rounded top. Rounded arches were characteristic of the Romanesque period. Pointed arches were characteristic of the Gothic period.

portcullis A heavy door, often made of metal, which is made to slide down at a castle's entrance in order to provide an extra defense.

relic A precious fragment, perhaps a bone or a piece of clothing, that was believed to belong to a saint or even to Jesus himself.

scullion A kitchen servant who cleaned dishes and did the less important (and more unpleasant) work of the cooks.

tracery Elaborate patterns of stone and glass at the tops of cathedral or church windows.

transept The "arms" of a cruciform cathedral.

trebuchet A gigantic wooden device designed to fling boulders into a castle.

For More Information

Columbia University Medieval Guild
602 Philosophy Hall
Columbia University
New York, NY 10027
e-mail: cal36@columbia.edu
Web site: http://www.cc.columbia.edu/cu/medieval

Dante Society of America
Brandeis University
MS 024
P.O. Box 549110
Waltham, MA 02454-9110
e-mail: dsa@dantesociety.org
Web site: http://www.dantesociety.org/index.html

International Courtly Literature Society
North American Branch
c/o Ms. Sara Sturm-Maddox
Department of French and Italian
University of Massachusetts at Amherst
Amherst, MA 01003
e-mail: ssmaddox@frital.umass.edu
Web site: http://wwwdept.usm.edu/~engdept/
   icls/iclsnab.htm

Medieval Academy of America
1430 Massachusetts Avenue
Cambridge, MA 02138
(617) 491-1622
e-mail: speculum@medievalacademy.org
Web site: http://www.medievalacademy.org/t_bar_2.htm

Rocky Mountain Medieval and Renaissance Association
Department of English Language and Literature
University of Northern Iowa
Cedar Falls, IA 50614-0502
(319) 273-2089
e-mail: jesse.swan@uni.edu
Web site: http://www.uni.edu/~swan/rmmra/rocky.htm

Web Sites

Due to the changing nature of Internet links, the Rosen Publishing Group, Inc., has developed an online list of Web sites related to the subject of this book. This site is updated regularly. Please use this link to access the list:

http://www.rosenlinks.com/lma/caca

For Further Reading

Bergin, Mark. *Castle*. London: Hodder Wayland, 2001.

Blair, John, and Joyce Cowley. *The Cathedrals of England*. Edinburgh and London: W. R. Chambers, Ltd., 1967.

Clifton-Taylor, Alec. *The Cathedrals of England*. London: Thames and Hudson, 1967.

Cruwys, Elizabeth, and Beau Riffenburgh. *Cathedrals of the World*. Basingstoke, UK: AA Publishing, 1997.

Felton, Herbert, and John Harvey. *The English Cathedrals*. London: B. T. Batsford Ltd., 1950.

Gravett, Christopher. *Castle* (Eyewitness Guides). London: Dorling Kindersley Ltd., 1994.

Macdonald, Fiona, and Mark Bergin. *A Medieval Castle*. London: Hodder Wayland, 2001.

McAleavy, Tony. *Life in a Medieval Castle*. London: English Heritage Publications, 1997.

McNeill, Sarah. *The Middle Ages*. Hove, UK: Macdonald Young Books, 1998.

Noonan, Damien. *Castles and Ancient Monuments of England*. London: Aurum Press, 1999.

Bibliography

Erlande-Brandenburg, Alain. *Cathedrals and Castles: Building in the Middle Ages*. New York: Harry N. Abrams, 1997.

Fletcher, Sir Banister, and Dan Cruikshank, ed. *A History of Architecture*, twentieth edition. London: Architectural Press (Butterworth-Heinemann), 1996.

Fry, Plantagenet Somerset. *Castles of Britain and Ireland*. London: David & Charles, 1996.

Icher, Francois, and Anthony Zielonka, trans. *Building the Great Cathedrals*. New York: Harry N. Abrams, 1998.

Martindale, Andrew. *Gothic Art*. London: Thames and Hudson, 1967.

Snyder, James. *Painting, Sculpture, Architecture, 4th–14th Century*. New York: Harry N. Abrams, 1998.

Toman, Rolf, ed. *The Art of Gothic*. Cologne, Germany: Könemann, 1999.

Index

A

apse, 33, 46
arch, 37, 39

B

basilica, 32, 33
Beaumaris Castle, 13, 28
bishop, 32, 33, 35, 44, 49
buttress, 39, 45, 49, 53

C

Caernarvon Castle, 14, 28
Caerphilly Castle, 28–29
campanile, 46, 51
Canterbury Cathedral, 46, 47
castles
  attacking, 7–8, 9, 21–22
  concentric, 9, 13
  day-to-day life in, 16–19
  defending, 7–8, 9, 13–15, 17, 21, 31
  design of, 7–15
  locations of, 8, 13–14, 28
  motte and bailey, 7–8, 9, 11, 24
  occupants of, 16–19
cathedrals
  activities in, 44–45
  dean of, 44
  design of, 32–34, 37–39, 41–43, 45–47
  orientation of, 33
  parts of, 45–47
chapter house, 44, 46

Charlemagne, 50
Chartres Cathedral, 38, 45, 46, 49
choir, 44–46
Christians, 31, 32–33, 44, 45, 47, 51
crown jewels, 24, 27
Crusades, 9, 21

D

diocese, 32, 34, 44, 47–49
Dover Castle, 10, 11, 26
Durham Cathedral, 35–37, 47, 49

E

Edinburgh Castle, 26–27
Edward I, 8–9, 13, 24, 28, 29
Elizabeth I, 24, 27
Ely Cathedral, 35, 41, 47
England, 9, 10, 27, 30, 43, 47
  castles of, 8, 10, 24–26
  cathedrals of, 33–37, 38–39, 41, 43, 46, 47–49, 51

F

finial, 45, 52
France, 16, 26
  castles of, 29–30
  cathedrals of, 37–38, 45, 47, 49–50, 51

G

gatehouse, 13, 14

Germany, 16, 26
  castles of, 30
  cathedrals of, 47, 50–51
Gothic architecture, 35, 37–43, 45,
      49, 51, 52
  decorated, 41, 43
  English, 39, 41, 43
  perpendicular, 41–43
Great Britain, 5, 9, 16

H

Hastings, Battle of, 5, 21
Henry II, 11, 26
Henry III, 8–9, 24
Henry VIII, 24, 49

I

Italy, cathedrals of, 51–52

J

James I, 26–27
James of St. George, Master, 13, 28

K

keep, 9, 10, 11, 13, 24, 26
Krak des Chevaliers, 9

L

lancet, 37, 39
Leaning Tower of Pisa, 46, 51

M

moat, 13, 14, 30
Montfort, Simon de, 8–9
Moors, 30–31, 52
Muslims, 9, 30

N

nave, 39, 43, 45, 46, 50
Normans, 5, 8, 9, 10, 24, 26, 29, 37
  architecture of, 34–35
Notre Dame Cathedral, 37, 39, 45, 49

O

Old Sarum, 35, 38

P

palisade, 7, 8, 11
pilgrims, 47, 53
prisoners, 22, 24, 37

R

Renaissance architecture, 51
Romanesque architecture, 33–37, 49, 53
Rome/Romans, 10, 26, 32, 33, 49,
      50, 53

S

Salisbury Cathedral, 38–39, 43,
      45, 49
Saxons, 5, 35, 49
Scotland, 9, 35, 37
  castles of, 26–27
Spain
  castles of, 30–31
  cathedrals of, 52–53
spire and tower, of cathedral, 35, 45,
      49, 50, 51, 52–53
stained glass, 46, 49

T

tombs, 47, 50, 53
tower, of castle, 11, 13, 15, 24, 26, 30
Tower of London, 9–10, 11, 14,
      24, 29
tracery, 41, 43
transept, 39, 45, 46, 53

W

Wales, 9
  castles of, 13, 14, 28–29
weapons, 14, 15, 17, 21–22
Wells Cathedral, 41, 45, 47
William the Conqueror, 5, 10, 24, 29,
      34–35, 38, 49
Winchester Cathedral, 35, 43, 47, 49
Windsor Castle, 8, 24–26
World War II, 24, 26

Y

York Cathedral, 41, 47, 49

About the Author

David Hilliam was educated at both Oxford and Cambridge Universities and has taught history at schools in Salisbury, Winchester, Canterbury, London, and Versailles. He is passionately interested in the British monarchy. His books include *Kings, Queens, Bones, and Bastards*; *Monarchs, Murders, and Mistresses*; and his latest, *Crown, Orb, and Sceptre*, which is an account of all the British royal coronations. At present he lives and teaches in Dorset, England.

Photo Credits

Designer: Geri Fletcher; **Editor:** Jake Goldberg; **Photo Researcher:** Elizabeth Loving